BOOM SCIENCE

SOUND

Georgia Amson-Bradshaw

BOOM SCIENCE

SOUND

Georgia Amson-Bradshaw

PowerKiDS
press

Published in 2020 by The Rosen Publishing Group, Inc.
29 East 21st Street, New York, NY 10010

Cataloging-in-Publication Data

Names: Amson-Bradshaw, Georgia.
Title: Sound / Georgia Amson-Bradshaw.
Description: New York : PowerKids Press, 2020. | Series: Boom science |
Includes glossary and index.
Identifiers: ISBN 9781725303898 (pbk.) | ISBN 9781725303911 (library
bound) | ISBN 9781725303904 (6pack)
Subjects: LCSH: Sound--Juvenile literature. | Sound--Measurement--Juvenile
literature.
Classification: LCC QC225.5 A56 2020 | DDC 534--dc23

Series Editor: Georgia Amson-Bradshaw
Series Designer: Rocket Design (East Anglia) Ltd

Picture acknowledgements:
Images from Shutterstock.com: VectorPot 6, robuart 7, Visual Generation 7br,
Jut 8t, Robert Ang 8b, Zoulou_55 9br, jehsomwang 10, Wor Sang Jun 11t, Yuri
Schmidt 11c, Barghest 11b, CharacterFamily 14t, Fotos593 15t, Iconic Bestiary
15b, Andrew Rybalko 16r, NotionPic 16l, Jiri Perina 17b, subarashii21 18t,
Dashikka 18c, nut jindarat 18b, Visual Generation 19, SunshineVector 22t,
JpegPhotographerArtistIO 22b, alejik 23c, Visual Generation 23b, Ovchinnkov
Vladimir 26t, Africa Studio 27t, NattapolStudiO 27b
All illustrations on pages 12, 13, 20, 21, 24, 25 by Steve Evans

All design elements from Shutterstock.

Manufactured in the United States of America

CPSIA Compliance Information: Batch CSPK19: For Further Information contact Rosen Publishing,
New York, New York at 1-800-237-9932.

Glossary words are shown in bold.

CONTENTS

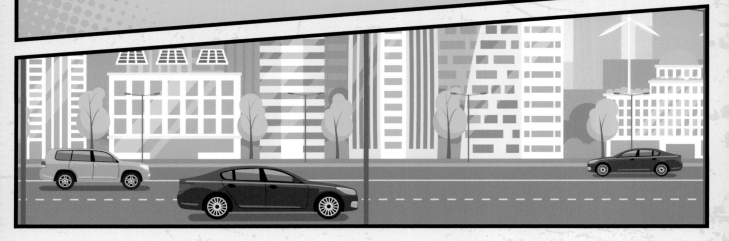

SOUND ALL AROUND

Sounds give us information about what is around us.

NOISY WORLD

Every day, we hear hundreds of different sounds. Some are loud, such as people shouting, or heavy trucks driving past. Others are quiet, such as a gentle breeze rustling the leaves on a tree.

BRMM

TALKING

We use sound to **communicate** with one another when we talk. We can make different words and sounds with our voices to tell each other things.

WARNINGS

Sound can be used to send out warnings. For example, the loud sound of an ambulance **siren** tells us a vehicle is coming through, and to get out of the way.

HIDE AND SEEK

We use electronic objects that make sound every day. Can you spot someone using one?

NEE NAW

NEE NAW

Wow!

MUSIC

People also enjoy sound for its own sake when they make and listen to **music**.

MOVING SOUND

Sound travels in waves of vibrations.

BUZZ

BUZZ

VIBRATIONS

Sounds are made by things vibrating, or moving backward and forward a tiny amount, very fast. For example, a bee's quickly vibrating wings are what makes its buzzing noise.

TRAVELING WAVES

Sounds travel because the vibrations spread out through the air in waves, like ripples in a pond. We hear sounds when the waves of vibrations reach our ears.

FEEL THE SOUND

Unlike ripples in a pond, most vibrations aren't easy to see. Try putting your hand on your throat and singing. The buzzing you will feel is your **vocal cords** vibrating to make the sound of your voice.

Do-re-mi-fah-so-la-ti-do!

WOW!

When we speak or sing, our vocal cords vibrate between 100 and 1,000 times per second, depending on the **pitch**.

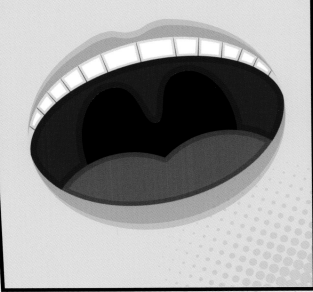

HEY, WHAT AM I?

Sounds are made when something vibrates. What can you see in this picture? Answer on page 28.

HEARING

We hear sounds when our ears sense vibrations.

 Sound waves travel through the air from a vibrating object.

HOW HEARING WORKS

inner ear

eardrum

middle ear

ear canal

outer ear

 Sound waves enter the ear and travel down the **ear canal** to the **eardrum**, which is a thin piece of skin.

 The eardrum passes the vibrations on to the **middle ear**, and then the **inner ear**. The inner ear is connected to the brain by **nerves**. The brain translates the vibrations into sounds that we hear.

10

EAR FLAPS

The part of your ears on the outside of your head is called the **outer ear**. It catches sound waves and directs them down the ear canal.

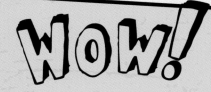

Snakes don't have outer ears. Instead they hear by sensing vibrations with their jawbones.

jawbone - - - - - - ->

HEY, WHAT AM I?
Listening to very loud music or other sounds can damage your ears, so sometimes it is necessary to protect them. What can you see in this picture? Answer on page 28.

YOUR TURN!

IMPROVE YOUR EARS

Some animals' hearing is better than ours. They have bigger ears, or ears they can move around. Try making some animal ears to improve your hearing. You'll need:

A roll of tape

Scissors

103.5

A radio or phone to play music

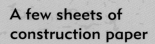

A few sheets of construction paper

STEP ONE

Make cone-shaped ears by rolling two pieces of construction paper into wide cones, and taping them in place. The small hole should rest in your outer ear, but don't push it into your ear canal.

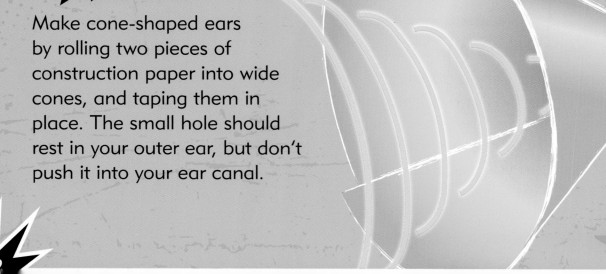

Make a second pair of ears by cutting two large teardrop shapes from construction paper. Cut a large triangle out of the bottom of each, then tape the cut sides together. This makes a cupped shape that you can hold behind your real ears to create extra large ears.

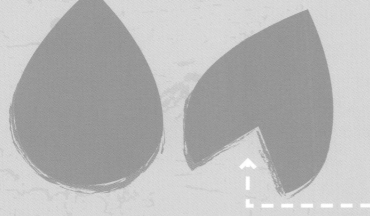

cut out triangle

Test out your ears by playing the music on your radio or phone on a very low **volume**. First, try the cone-shaped ears. Do they make the sound quieter or louder? Does it make a difference what direction the cones are pointing? Try the cupped ears. How do they compare? Does angling the cupped ears up or down make a difference?

13

LOUD AND QUIET SOUNDS

The volume of a sound is how loud or quiet it is.

WOO YEAH! LET'S ROCK!

BANG!

BOOM!

BIG VIBRATIONS

Loud sounds make big vibrations. When a drummer hits a drum hard and the skin vibrates back and forth a lot, this makes a loud bang.

Do you have to hit so hard? My ears are ringing!

SMALL VIBRATIONS

A drummer gently tapping a drum makes a quieter noise because the vibrations of the drum are small.

LOUDER GOES FURTHER

The louder a noise is, the further it will travel. The rumble of a thunderstorm or a volcano erupting can be heard from several miles away, but a whisper is too quiet to be heard across a room.

DECIBELS

The volume of a sound is measured in **decibels**. A quiet whisper is about 30 decibels. A TV is around 70 decibels. A vacuum cleaner's sound is about 75 decibels.

VRRRRMM

Ugh, Mom, now I can't hear the TV!

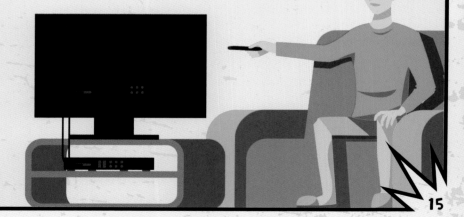

HIGH AND LOW SOUNDS

The pitch of a sound is how high or low it is.

FAST VIBRATIONS

Some sounds, such as a whistle being blown, or a bird tweeting, have a high pitch. The vibrations of a high-pitched sound are very fast.

TWEET

TWEET

WHISTLE

GRRRRRR!!!

SLOW VIBRATIONS

Sounds such as the rumble of thunder or a dog's growl are low-pitched sounds. The vibrations of these sounds are slower.

HIDE AND SEEK

People's voices have different pitches. Can you spot a person who might have a high-pitched voice? Answer on page 28.

TWANG

TWANG

PITCH IN ACTION

Twang a ruler on the edge of a table. When the ruler is mostly off the table, the vibrations are slow and the pitch is low. What happens when the ruler is mostly on the table?

WOW!

Young people can hear higher-pitched sounds than adults. Some clever teenagers created a mobile phone ringtone that they could hear, but their teachers couldn't!

MUSIC

We make special sounds using musical instruments.

NICE NOISES

People like to listen to music. It can make us feel lots of different **emotions**.

Lovely moo-sic!

WOW!

Some animals seem to enjoy music, too. An experiment showed that cows made more milk when listening to music, because they were calmer.

HEY, WHAT AM I?

The inside of which well-known instrument is shown in this picture? Answer on page 29.

HOW INSTRUMENTS WORK

Instruments make sounds by vibrating the air around them at different pitches to make different **notes**.

Wind instruments make sounds when air is blown into them. The air inside them vibrates and makes notes.

String instruments are plucked or scraped with a bow. The strings vibrate and air inside the wooden body vibrates, making the sounds louder.

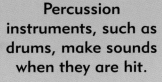

Percussion instruments, such as drums, make sounds when they are hit.

FORM A BAND

Get a couple of friends together and play music on your own DIY string instrument, percussion instrument, and wind instrument. You'll need:

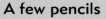

A few pencils

An uninflated balloon

An empty metal can

A plastic drinking straw

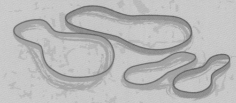
A selection of medium and large rubber bands

Scissors

A cardboard tissue box

STEP ONE

Cut the bendy part off the drinking straw. Flatten the end and snip the tip into a pointed shape. Put the snipped end into your mouth and seal your lips around it. Try blowing harder and softer until you can get the straw to make a noise like an oboe.

FRONT VIEW   SIDE VIEW

Snip these parts off

STEP TWO

Cut the narrow end off the balloon. Ask an adult to help you stretch the round part of the balloon over the top of the empty metal can. Be careful of sharp edges! This makes a drum that you can play with your fingers, or using pencils as drumsticks.

STEP THREE

Stretch a selection of rubber bands lengthways around an empty tissue box. Choose bands with different thicknesses, which will play at different pitches. Slide a pencil between the rubber bands and the box just before the hole to create a **bridge**. Your instruments are complete! With your friends, play your instruments to make a tune.

SOUND AND MATERIALS

Sound travels better through some materials than others.

Who wants fish for dinner?

SOLIDS AND LIQUIDS

Sound doesn't just travel through air. It travels through **solids**, such as wood, and **liquids**, such as water, too.

Gulp!

HEY, WHAT AM I?
Sound travels more easily through some **materials** than others. Metal pipes carry sound well, but sound waves cannot pass as easily through this material. What is it? Answer on page 29.

WHERE SOUND GOES

There are three things that can happen to a sound when it hits a new material:

1 Sound is **reflected**. It bounces back off the hard surface (see pages 26 and 27).

2 Sound passes through. Some materials let the sound wave partly pass through. This is how we can hear sounds through walls or windows.

3 Some materials **absorb** sound like a sponge, and stop it from passing through. This is how we can use materials such as foam in headphones to block sounds out.

HEAR SECRET SOUNDS

Discover how sound travels through solids with this experiment. You'll need:

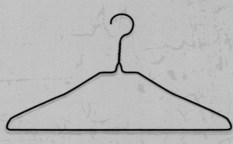

A wire coat hanger

1-foot-long (0.3 m) piece of string

Objects made of other materials, such as a large plastic spoon or wooden tongs

STEP ONE

Tie the hook of the wire coat hanger in the center of your piece of string. Wrap the ends of the string around your fingers. Holding the coat hanger up, allow it to swing against a chair or wall. Listen carefully. Can you hear a sound?

STEP TWO

With the ends of the string still wrapped around your fingers, put your fingers on the flaps just in front of your ear canal. This closes off your ear canal without you putting your fingers inside your ears. Allow the coat hanger to swing against a chair or wall again. How does it sound this time?

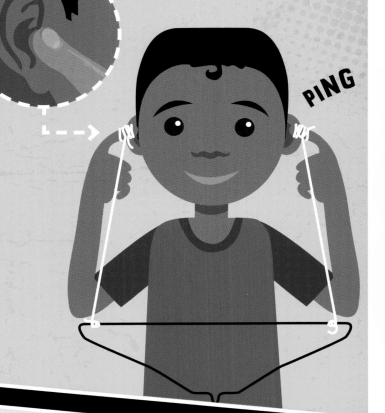

PING

STEP THREE

TWANG

Tie the string to objects made of different materials, such as a pair of wooden tongs, and repeat the experiment again. Why do you think the sounds are different when you listen to them through the string? Answer on page 29.

ECHOES

An echo is made by sound bouncing off a surface.

TWEET

BOUNCING SOUND

Sound waves travel away from whatever is making them. When sound waves hit a hard surface, some are reflected and bounce back again.

ECHO, ECHO

If you shout inside a large, rocky cave, you'll hear your words repeated back. This is an **echo** made by the sound bouncing off the hard walls and traveling back to you.

HELLO

HELLO

HELLO

ECHO INGREDIENTS

In order to make an echo, the hard surface must be far enough away for us to hear the bounced sound separately from the original noise, and there must be no soft surfaces to absorb the sound.

No echoes in here.

I can see you ... with my ears!

WOW!

Bats use echoes to find bugs to eat in the dark. They make high-pitched noises, and their powerful hearing tells them where the sound is bouncing back from. This is called **echolocation**.

HIDE AND SEEK

Other animals also use echolocation to hunt. Can you spot one? Answer on page 29.

ANSWERS

Page 7

Hide and Seek A woman talking on a cell phone

Page 9

What am I? I'm a guitar string vibrating after being plucked.

Page 11

What am I?
I'm a pair of headphones for blocking loud noises.

Page 17

Hide and Seek A young child. Children have higher-pitched voices than adults.

Page 18

What am I?

I'm a piano. Pianos make sound using small hammers that are attached to the keys, which hit strings.

Page 22

What am I? I'm cotton balls.

Page 25

Your turn

We normally hear sounds when the sound waves travel through the air and reach our ears. But air is not the best material for carrying sound. The string carries the vibrations from the hanger to your ear better than the air, and so you hear a louder noise. The different materials also sound different from one another because some materials vibrate more than others when they are hit.

Page 27

Hide and Seek A dolphin. Dolphins also use echolocation to hunt for fish.

GLOSSARY

absorb to soak up

communicate to tell one another things

bridge part of an instrument that supports the strings

decibel a unit of measurement for the loudness of a sound

ear canal the passage in your ear that runs from the outside of your head to your eardrum

eardrum a thin piece of skin inside your ear that receives vibrations from sound waves

echo a repeated noise caused when sound bounces off a surface

echolocation a way of using bounced sound waves to sense where something is

emotions feelings, such as happiness or sadness

inner ear the part of the ear furthest inside the head that sends the sounds we hear to the brain

liquid a material, such as water, that flows and does not hold its shape

material the stuff that something is made of

middle ear the part of the ear that passes sound waves from the ear canal to the inner ear

music sounds made by people or instruments that are nice to listen to

nerves thin pathways that send information around the body

note a musical sound with a particular pitch

outer ear the bit of the ear on the outside of the head

pitch how high or low a sound is

reflect to bounce back off a surface

siren something that makes a loud warning sound

solid a hard material that holds its shape

vocal cords flaps of skin in the throat that vibrate and produce sounds

volume how loud or quiet a sound is

FURTHER INFORMATION

Books

Clark, Michael. *Strange Science and Explosive Experiments: Shattering Sounds*. New York, NY: Rosen Publishing Group, 2018.

Loria, Laura. *Let's Find Out! Forms of Energy: What Is Sound Energy?* New York, NY: Britannica Educational Publishing, 2018.

Riley, Peter. *Moving Up with Science: Sound*. New York, NY: PowerKids Press, 2017.

Websites

Brain Pop

www.brainpop.com/science/energy/sound/

Britannica Kids

kids.britannica.com/kids/article/sound/353791

National Geographic Kids

www.kids.nationalgeographic.com/explore/youtube-playlist-pages/youtube-playlist-sound/

Publisher's note to educators and parents: Our editors have carefully reviewed these websites to ensure that they are suitable for students. Many websites change frequently, however, and we cannot guarantee that a site's future contents will continue to meet our high standards of quality and educational value. Be advised that students should be closely supervised whenever they access the Internet.

INDEX